GOOD
FLIGHT
ANTELOPE
VALLEY
BY THE J. YOUNG FAMILY

DEDICATION

**FOR OUR FRIEND MRS. NYLA USSERY,
WHO ENCOURAGES OUR MINDS TO DISCOVER MORE BY READING
AND ASKING LOTS OF QUESTIONS.**

COPYRIGHT © 2017 JOHNNY YOUNG JR.
ALL RIGHTS RESERVED.
ISBN: 10: 1981286950
ISBN-13: 978-1981286959

"A FAMILY THAT CREATES TOGETHER STAYS TOGETHER"
"THIS LITTLE LIGHT – WE WILL LET IT SHINE"
"THANK YOU LORD!"
-THE J. YOUNGS

on...
art impacting culture

CALIFORNIA JUNIPER

FAR ABOVE THE JUNIPER HILLS

2 CALIFORNIA POPPY

WHERE THE SUN SHINES BRIGHT
ABOVE CALIFORNIA POPPY FIELDS

4 RINGNECK DOVE

WHERE QUIET DOVES
MAKE A HOUSE A HOME

6 JOSHUA TREE

AND JOSHUA TREES ARE
VERY WELL KNOWN

A SPLASH OF CITY LIFE
NEVER DOES BOTHER

THE PLUMP BABY QUAIL
AND HIS PROUD QUAIL FATHER

11 CALIFORNIA QUAIL

WHERE SUNSETS AND ROLLING HILLS GO PERFECTLY TOGETHER

14 RED-TAIL HAWK

LOOK CAREFULLY ABOVE
AND SEE BEAUTIFUL BROWN HAWKS
WITH RED TAIL FEATHERS

NOT MUCH RAIN
WITH PLENTY OF DESERT LANDSCAPE
AND DRY HEAT

THE PERFECT INVITATION
FOR THE ANNUAL
SOUTH FLIGHT OF GEESE

17 SNOW GEESE MIGRATION

WHERE THE CRAFTY COYOTE TROT IN A RUSH

Gov. Edmund G. "Pat" Brown
California
Aqueduct
STATE WATER PROJECT

OFF THE BEATEN PATH
RIGHT NEAR THE
CALIFORNIA AQUEDUCT

AND SHINY BLACK RAVENS
RACE NON-STOP

TO REACH THE FOURTY-FIVE
DEGREE ANGLES OF
VASQUEZ ROCKS

HAVE A GOOD FLIGHT DOVES
HAVE A GOOD FLIGHT QUAILS
HAVE A GOOD FLIGHT HAWKS
HAVE A GOOD FLIGHT GEESE
HAVE A GOOD FLIGHT RAVENS
HAVE A GOOD FLIGHT
ANTELOPE VALLEY

THE END

www.ingramcontent.com/pod-product-compliance
Lightning Source LLC
Chambersburg PA
CBHW040208240726
48664CB00002B/876